BEHIND CLOSED DOORS

Navigating the Unspoken Challenges of Special Needs

MARK TAYLOR

Mark Taylor
Behind Closed Doors: Navigating the Unspoken Challenges of Special Needs

Published by Spines
ISBN: 979-8-89383-431-4

Spines

Our Story

Hello, I'm Mark Taylor. My wife and I have a 9-year-old son, Mark Jr., who is dually diagnosed with Down syndrome, ADHD, and autism. Mark Jr. is also a wanderer (Eloper), requiring 24-hour care due to safety factors we encounter. We're on a journey of embracing the unique challenges and joys of raising him. However, our journey didn't come with a manual. We had to navigate uncertainties and figure things out as we went along. In the beginning, we faced frustration with limited resources and no clear direction. We understand the overwhelming feeling of starting such a journey without answers.

This guide aims to provide insights based on our experiences. We acknowledge that every child is a case study of their own, but these are general nuggets that aren't often discussed. After reading this guide, we hope you'll feel better equipped to embark on your journey.

Additionally, we offer a free parent empowerment video program to provide further support on your path. Remember, you're not alone. "Behind Closed Doors" is here to help!

Introduction

Welcome to "Behind Closed Doors," a comprehensive guide designed to support and uplift parents raising exceptional children. This e-guide is crafted to provide valuable insights, practical tips, and resources to help you navigate the unique journey of parenting special needs individuals.

Contents

1

Understanding Special Needs

Definition of Special Needs:

Special needs refer to the unique requirements of individuals who experience challenges that may arise from physical, intellectual, emotional, or developmental conditions. These needs necessitate additional support, accommodations, or tailored interventions to ensure individuals can participate fully in various aspects of life.

Diversity of Special Needs:

Special needs encompass a broad spectrum, including but not limited to:

- Intellectual Disabilities: Challenges in intellectual functioning and adaptive behaviors.

- Physical Disabilities: Limitations in mobility or coordination.

- Sensory Impairments: Difficulties with vision, hearing, or other sensory functions.

- Emotional/Behavioral Disorders: Conditions affecting emotional well-being and behavior regulation.

- Developmental Disorders: Delays or differences in milestones and skills acquisition.

Common Challenges:

1. Access to Education: Ensuring inclusive educational environments and tailored learning approaches.

2. Social Stigma: Overcoming stereotypes and fostering a more inclusive society.

3. Healthcare Disparities: Addressing healthcare inequalities and specialized medical care.

4. Limited Accessibility: Physical and social barriers that hinder full participation.

5. Financial Strain: Additional costs associated with therapies, assistive devices, and specialized education.

Misconceptions:

1. One Size Fits All: Understanding that each individual's needs are unique, and interventions should be personalized.

2. Limitations vs. Potential: Recognizing the abilities and potential for growth in individuals with special needs.

3. Inability to Contribute: Appreciating Appreciate the diverse talents and contributions individuals with special needs bring to communities.

4. Uniform Experience: Acknowledging the variability in experiences and challenges among individuals with special needs.

In fostering understanding, it's crucial to embrace the diversity within the special needs community and dispel common misconceptions, promoting a more inclusive and supportive environment for all.

Short Story: Emma's Journey to Empowerment

Emma, a mother of a child with Down syndrome, felt isolated and overwhelmed after receiving her son's diagnosis. Unsure of where to turn for support, she decided to attend a local support group for parents of children with special needs. There, she met other parents who shared their experiences, offered guidance, and became a source of comfort and understanding.

One of the parents she met, Sarah, shared her journey of advocating for her daughter, who had autism. Sarah talked about the challenges she faced in getting the right support and services for her daughter, from navigating the education system to finding therapists who understood her daughter's needs. She also shared the joy she felt when her daughter achieved milestones that many had thought impossible.

Through Sarah's story, Emma gained valuable insights into the importance of advocacy and perseverance when it comes to raising a child with special needs. She also learned about the importance of building a support network and connecting with others who understand the unique joys and challenges of special parenting.

Inspired by Sarah's story, Emma became more proactive in seeking out resources and support for her son. She joined advocacy groups, attended workshops and seminars, and connected with other parents in her community. With the support of her new network, Emma felt more empowered and better equipped to navigate the challenges of raising a child with special needs.

Emma's experience highlights the importance of sharing stories and experiences within the special needs community. By connecting with others and learning from their experiences, parents like Emma can gain valuable insights and support that can help them on their journey.

2

Embracing Your Role

Nurturing a Positive Mindset:

1. Focus on Abilities: Shift your perspective from challenges to abilities, celebrating achievements no matter how small.

2. Self-Compassion: Acknowledge that it's okay to face difficulties and take time for self-care without guilt.

3. Build a Support Network: Surround yourself with understanding friends, family, and support groups to share experiences and insights.

4. Set Realistic Goals: Break down larger goals into manageable steps, recognizing progress along the way.

Advocacy and Collaboration with Professionals:

1. Know Your Rights: Familiarize yourself with laws and policies that protect the rights of individuals with special needs in education, healthcare, and employment.

2. Effective Communication: Establish open and honest communication with educators, healthcare providers, and other professionals involved in your child's life.

3. Educate Others: Advocate for awareness and under-

standing within your community to foster a more inclusive environment.

4. Collaborate with Professionals: Work collaboratively with therapists, teachers, and specialists to create a cohesive support system for your child.

5. Stay Informed: Stay updated on the latest research, therapies, and resources relevant to your child's needs.

Embracing your role involves fostering a positive mindset that focuses on strengths and possibilities. Advocacy and collaboration with professionals are essential aspects of ensuring that your child receives the support and resources necessary for their growth and well-being. Together, these elements contribute to a more empowered and resilient journey for both you and your child.

Short Story: Finding Strength in Community

Alex, a father of a child with autism, initially felt overwhelmed and isolated after his son's diagnosis. He didn't know where to turn for support or how to navigate the challenges that lay ahead. However, everything changed when he attended a local support group for parents of children with special needs.

At the support group, Alex met other parents who shared their experiences, offered guidance, and provided much-needed support. He learned about the importance of self-care, advocacy, and collaboration with professionals. He also discovered that he was not alone and that there were others who understood the unique joys and challenges of raising a child with special needs.

One of the parents he met, James, shared his experience of advocating for his daughter, who had ADHD. James talked about the challenges he faced in getting the right support and services for his daughter, from navigating the education system to finding therapists who understood her needs. He also shared the joy he felt when his daughter achieved milestones that many had thought impossible.

Through James's story, Alex gained valuable insights into the importance of finding strength in the community and connecting with others who understand the unique journey of special parenting. Inspired by James's story, Alex became more proactive in seeking out resources and support for his own son. He joined advocacy groups, attended workshops and seminars, and connected with other parents in his community. With the support of his new network, Alex felt more empowered and better equipped to navigate the challenges of raising a child with special needs.

Alex's experience highlights the importance of sharing stories and experiences within the special needs community. By connecting with others and learning from their experiences, parents like Alex can gain valuable insights and support that can help them on their journey.

3

Building a Support System

Connecting with Other Parents:

1. Join Support Groups: Seek out local or online support groups specifically tailored to parents of special needs individuals.

2. Attend Workshops and Events: Participate in workshops, seminars, and events focused on special needs parenting to share experiences and gain insights.

3. Social Media Communities: Explore online platforms where parents discuss challenges, share resources, and offer encouragement.

Engaging with Local Communities and Organizations:

1. Community Events: Attend local events or activities that bring families together, fostering a sense of community.

2. School Involvement: Engage with your child's school community through parent-teacher associations or special education committees.

3. Volunteer Opportunities: Contribute your time and

skills to organizations supporting individuals with special needs, and creating connections with like-minded individuals.

4. Collaborate with Local Businesses: Partner with local businesses to create inclusive spaces and opportunities for special needs individuals.

Building a robust support system involves not only connecting with fellow parents but also actively engaging with local communities and organizations. These connections provide valuable resources, shared experiences, and a sense of belonging that can significantly enhance your journey as a parent of a special needs individual.

Short Story: Sarah's Path to Advocacy

Sarah, a mother of a child with cerebral palsy, felt lost and overwhelmed after her daughter's diagnosis. She didn't know where to turn for support or how to navigate the challenges that lay ahead. However, everything changed when she attended a local support group for parents of children with special needs.

At the support group, Sarah met other parents who shared their experiences, offered guidance, and provided much-needed support. She learned about the importance of self-care, advocacy, and collaboration with professionals. She also discovered that she was not alone and that there were others whoothers others understood the unique joys and challenges of raising a child with special needs.

One of the parents she met, Lisa, shared her experience of advocating for her son, who had dyslexia. Lisa talked about the challenges she faced in getting the right support and services for her son, from navigating the education system to finding tutors who understood his needs. She also shared the joy she felt when her son achieved milestones that many had thought impossible.

Through Lisa's story, Sarah gained valuable insights into the importance of finding her voice as an advocate and connecting with others who understand the unique journey of special parenting. Inspired by Lisa's story, Sarah became more proactive in seeking out resources and support for her own daughter. She joined advocacy groups, attended workshops and seminars, and connected with other parents in her community. With the support of her new network, Sarah felt more empowered and better equipped to navigate the challenges of raising a child with special needs.

Sarah's experience highlights the importance of sharing stories and experiences within the special needs community. By connecting with others and learning from their experiences, parents like Sarah can gain valuable insights and support that can help them on their journey.

4

Educational Strategies
TAILORING LEARNING EXPERIENCES

UNDERSTANDING YOUR CHILD'S NEEDS:

Understanding your child's unique learning style and needs is crucial for tailoring educational experiences effectively. Take the time to observe how they respond to different teaching methods, environments, and types of interaction. This observation will guide you in creating a personalized learning plan that maximizes their your potential for growth and development.

INDIVIDUALIZED EDUCATION PLAN (IEP):

An Individualized Education Plan (IEP) is a personalized roadmap for your child's educational journey. It outlines specific learning goals, accommodations, and support services tailored to their needs. Work closely with your child's teachers, therapists, and school administrators to develop and regularly review the IEP, ensuring it evolves with your child's progress and changing needs.

MULTISENSORY LEARNING:

Many special needs children benefit from multisensory learning experiences that engage multiple senses simultaneously. Incorporate hands-on activities, visual aids, music, movement, and other sensory experiences into your child's learning to enhance engagement and comprehension.

Structured Learning Environment:

Create a structured and predictable learning environment to help your child feel safe, secure, and focused. Establish consistent routines, clear expectations, and visual schedules to minimize anxiety and support their understanding of daily activities and transitions.

Positive Reinforcement:

Utilize positive reinforcement techniques to motivate and reward your child's progress and achievements. Praise their efforts, celebrate their successes, and use rewards that are meaningful to them. Positive reinforcement not only encourages desired behaviors but also boosts self-confidence and self-esteem.

5

Effective Communication with Educators

Establishing Open Communication:

Open and honest communication between parents and educators is essential for supporting your child's educational journey. Establish a collaborative partnership with your child's teachers and school staff, sharing insights into your child's strengths, challenges, and preferences.

Regular Progress Updates:

Schedule regular meetings with your child's teachers to discuss their progress, challenges, and any necessary adjustments to their learning plan. These check-ins provide an opportunity to address concerns proactively and ensure everyone remains aligned with your child's educational goals.

Advocating for Your Child:

Be an active advocate for your child's educational needs, ensuring they receive the support and accommodations necessary for their success. Familiarize yourself with relevant laws and policies, such as the Individuals with Disabilities Education Act (IDEA), and assertively communicate your child's rights to appropriate educational services and accommodations.

Collaborative Problem-Solving:

Approach challenges collaboratively, working together with educators to identify solutions and strategies that support your child's learning and well-being. Share insights from home and seek input from school professionals to develop a comprehensive support plan that addresses your child's academic, social, and emotional needs.

Empowering Your Child:

Encourage your child to participate actively in their education, fostering a sense of ownership and empowerment. Teach them self-advocacy skills, such as asking for help when needed, communicating their needs, and actively participating in their IEP meetings as appropriate.

Short Story: A Personalized Learning Journey

When my son, David, was diagnosed with autism spectrum disorder (ASD) at the age of four, my wife and I were unsure how to navigate his educational journey. David struggled with communication, social interaction, and sensory processing, making traditional classroom settings challenging for him.

We decided to work closely with David's school to develop an Individualized Education Plan (IEP) tailored to his unique needs. Together with his teachers and therapists, we created a structured learning environment that incorporated multisensory activities, visual schedules, and positive reinforcement strategies.

One of the most impactful changes we made was introducing a sensory corner in David's classroom where he could retreat when feeling overwhelmed. This safe space, equipped with soft lighting, comfortable seating, and sensory toys, allowed David to self-regulate and refocus, improving his ability to participate in classroom activities.

Through open communication with David's educators, we identified his strengths and areas for growth, adjusting his learning plan as needed. Regular progress updates and collaborative problem-solving meetings ensured that everyone involved in David's education remained aligned and supportive.

As David progressed through elementary school, we saw remarkable improvements in his confidence, communication skills, and academic performance. With the right support and a personalized learning approach, David blossomed into a curious and engaged learner, eager to explore the world around him.

Today, David is a thriving teenager who enjoys learning, socializing with his peers, and pursuing his interests. His journey is a testament to the power of personalized education and the importance of collaboration between parents and educators in supporting special needs children.

6

Collaborate with Professionals for a Cohesive Support System

1. Open Communication: Establish clear and open lines of communication with your child's therapists, teachers, and specialists to ensure everyone is on the same page regarding goals and strategies.

2. Regular Updates: Schedule regular meetings or check-ins to receive updates on your child's progress, discuss any concerns, and adjust interventions as needed.

3. Share Insights: Provide insights into your child's strengths, challenges, and preferences to help professionals tailor their approaches and better understand your child's unique needs.

4. Attend Meetings and Workshops: Participate in school meetings, workshops, and training sessions to stay informed about the latest developments in special education and therapeutic approaches.

5. Collaborative Goal Setting: Work together to set realistic and achievable goals for your child's development, considering both academic and personal growth.

6. Incorporate Home Strategies: Collaborate on strategies

that can be implemented at home to reinforce learning and support your child's progress outside of structured sessions.

7. Advocate for Resources: Collaborate with professionals to identify and access appropriate resources, accommodations, and support services that can enhance your child's educational and therapeutic experience.

Remember, a collaborative approach involving parents and professionals creates a more comprehensive and effective support system for the overall well-being and development of your child.

Short Story: The Power of Collaboration

When Emily's son, Jake, was diagnosed with autism, she was overwhelmed by the challenges that lay ahead. She didn't know where to turn for support or how to ensure that Jake received the best possible care and education. However, everything changed when she met Dr. Patel, a specialist in autismn autism specialist who became an invaluable source of support and guidance.

Dr. Patel took the time to listen to Emily's concerns and answer her questions. He provided valuable insights into Jake's condition and recommended a range of therapies and interventions that could help him thrive. He also introduced Emily to a network of professionals who could support Jake's development, from speech therapists to behavioral specialists.

With Dr. Patel's guidance, Emily was able to develop a comprehensive support plan for Jake that addressed his unique needs and challenges. She worked closely with Jake's teachers to ensure that he received the accommodations and support he needed to succeed in school. She also connected with other parents of children with autism, who provided invaluable advice and support.

Thanks to the power of collaboration, Jake made great strides in his development. He learned to communicate more effectively, regulate his emotions, and interact with others in a positive waypositively interact with otherspositively interact with others. Emily was amazed by the progress he made and grateful for the support she received along the way.

Emily's story is a powerful reminder of the importance of collaboration in supporting children with special needs. By working together with professionals, educators, and other parents, families can create a comprehensive support system that helps children like Jake reach their full potential.

7

Promoting Independence

DEVELOPING LIFE SKILLS AND ENCOURAGING SELF-EXPRESSION

Developing Life Skills:

1. Daily Routines: Foster independence by involving your child in daily routines, such as dressing, grooming, and meal preparation, tailored to their abilities.

2. Chores and Responsibilities: Assign age-appropriate chores and responsibilities, emphasizing the importance of contributing to the household and developing essential life skills.

3. Problem-Solving Activities: Encourage your child to engage in activities that require problem-solving, decision-making, and critical thinking to build confidence and autonomy.

Encouraging Self-Expression:

1. Artistic Outlets: Provide opportunities for creative expression through art, music, or other artistic pursuits, allowing your child to communicate and express themselves in diverse ways.

2. Journaling or Communication Devices: Introduce tools

like journals or communication devices to facilitate self-expression, especially if verbal communication is a challenge.

3. Choice Making: Offer choices whenever possible, empowering your child to make decisions and express preferences, promoting a sense of control over their own life.

4. Social Interactions: Facilitate social interactions with peers and encourage your child to express their thoughts and feelings in various social settings.

By focusing on developing life skills and encouraging self-expression, you empower your child to navigate the world with increased independence and confidence. Tailor these approaches to your child's unique abilities and preferences for the most effective results.

Short Story: Learning Through Play

When David's daughter, Emma, was diagnosed with Down syndrome, he was determined to help her live a happy, fulfilling life. He knew that Emma would face challenges along the way, but he was determined to provide her with the support and encouragement she needed to succeed.

One of the ways David helped Emma develop important life skills was through play. He created games and activities that were not only fun but also helped Emma learn important skills like counting, sorting, and following directions. For example, he would set up a scavenger hunt around the house, hiding objects for Emma to find and then helping her count them as she collected them.

David also encouraged Emma to express herself through art and music. He set up an art station in the living room, complete with paints, markers, and paper, and let Emma create whatever she wanted. He also introduced her to different musical instruments, like drums and keyboards, and encouraged her to experiment with different sounds and rhythms.

Thanks to David's support and encouragement, Emma developed important life skills and learned to express herself in creative ways. She became more independent and confident, and David couldn't have been prouder of her accomplishments.

David's story is a powerful reminder of the importance of learning through play. By creating fun and engaging activities that promote learning and self-expression, parents can help their children develop important skills and build confidence and independence.

8

Coping Strategies for Parents

STRESS MANAGEMENT AND BALANCING SELF-CARE

Stress Management:

1. Identify Stressors: Recognize and understand specific stressors related to parenting a child with special needs.

2. Mindfulness and Relaxation Techniques: Practice mindfulness, deep breathing, or meditation to reduce stress and promote emotional well-being.

3. Set Realistic Expectations: Establish achievable goals for yourself and your child, acknowledging that progress may occur at its own pace.

4. Seek Support: Build a network of support, including friends, family, or support groups, to share experiences and receive emotional support.

5. Professional Counseling: Consider seeking professional counseling or therapy to address stressors and build coping strategies.

Balancing Self-Care and Caregiving:

1. Schedule "Me Time": Allocate dedicated time for self-care activities, whether it's reading, exercising, or pursuing hobbies, to recharge and maintain personal well-being.

2. Delegate Responsibilities: Share caregiving responsibilities with trusted friends, family, or hired support to prevent burnout.

3. Set Boundaries: Establish clear boundaries between caregiving responsibilities and personal time to maintain a healthy balance.

4. Regular Health Checkups: Prioritize your physical and mental health by scheduling regular checkups and addressing any health concerns promptly.

5. Celebrate Small Wins: Acknowledge and celebrate both your achievements and those of your child, fostering a positive and rewarding caregiving experience.

Remember, taking care of yourself is vital to providing effective care for your child. Balancing stress management and self-care contributes to a healthier and more sustainable parenting journey.

Short Story: Finding Strength in Community

When Sarah's daughter, Lily, was diagnosed with cerebral palsy, Sarah felt like her world had been turned upside down. She was overwhelmed by the challenges that lay ahead and unsure of how to navigate this new reality. However, she soon discovered that she was not alone.

Sarah connected with other parents of children with cerebral palsy through a local support group. These parents became her lifeline, offering support, guidance, and encouragement as she navigated the ups and downs of parenting a child with special needs. They shared their experiences and insights, providing Sarah with valuable advice and helping her see that there was hope for the future.

With the support of her community, Sarah learned valuable coping strategies that helped her manage stress and prioritize self-care. She found solace in activities like yoga and meditation, which helped her stay grounded and focused during difficult times. She also made sure to carve out time for herself, whether it was going for a walk in the park or enjoying a quiet cup of tea.

Thanks to the support of her community and her dedication to self-care, Sarah was able to face the challenges of parenting a child with special needs with courage and resilience. She learned to celebrate the small wins and find joy in the everyday moments, knowing that she was not alone on this journey.

Sarah's story is a powerful reminder of the importance of finding strength in the community. By connecting with others who understand your experiences and challenges, you can find support, encouragement, and hope as you navigate the ups and downs of parenting a child with special needs.

9

Financial and Legal Guidance

ACCESSING RESOURCES AND UNDERSTANDING RIGHTS

ACCESSING AVAILABLE RESOURCES:

1. Research Assistance Programs: Explore government and community assistance programs that offer financial support, therapy services, and educational resources for families with special needs.

2. Nonprofit Organizations: Connect with nonprofit organizations dedicated to supporting individuals with special needs, as they often provide valuable resources and assistance.

3. Local Community Services: Investigate local community services, such as support groups, counseling services, and workshops, which may offer financial guidance and emotional support.

UNDERSTANDING RIGHTS AND BENEFITS:

1. Educate Yourself: Familiarize yourself with local and national laws regarding the rights of individuals with special needs, including educational rights, employment protections, and access to public services.

2. Individualized Education Plan (IEP): Understand the

process of developing an IEP for your child, ensuring their educational needs are properly addressed.

3. Legal Advocacy: If necessary, seek legal advice or advocacy to protect your child's rights, especially in areas such as disability discrimination or access to accommodations.

4. Social Security Benefits: Explore available social security benefits, including Supplemental Security Income (SSI) or Social Security Disability Insurance (SSDI), that may provide financial assistance.

By accessing available resources and understanding rights and benefits, you empower yourself to navigate the financial and legal aspects of caring for a child with special needs, ensuring they receive the support and opportunities they deserve.

Short Story: Navigating the Legal Maze

When James and Emily's son, Michael, was diagnosed with autism, they were thrust into a world of uncertainty and confusion. They were unsure of their rights and felt overwhelmed by the complexities of the legal system. However, with the help of an advocate and support group, they were able to navigate the legal maze and secure the resources their son needed to thrive.

James and Emily attended workshops and seminars to learn more about their rights as parents of a child with special needs. They familiarized themselves with laws such as the Individuals with Disabilities Education Act (IDEA) and the Americans with Disabilities Act (ADA), which protected Michael's rights to receive a free and appropriate education and access accommodations in public spaces.

With the support of their advocate, James and Emily were able to develop an Individualized Education Plan (IEP) that addressed Michael's unique needs and ensured he received the support and services necessary for his success in school. They also learned how to effectively advocate for their son's rights, whether it was requesting accommodations at school or fighting discrimination in the community.

Thanks to their newfound knowledge and support network, James and Emily felt empowered to navigate the legal system and secure the resources their son needed to thrive. They were grateful for the guidance and support they received and knew that they were not alone on this journey.

James and Emily's story is a powerful reminder of the importance of understanding your rights and advocating for your child. By educating yourself about the legal system and seeking support from advocates and support groups, you can navigate the complexities of the legal maze and secure the resources your child needs to succeed.

10

Creating Inclusive Environments

FOSTERING UNDERSTANDING IN THE COMMUNITY:

1. Educational Initiatives: Collaborate with local schools and educational institutions to implement programs that raise awareness about special needs and promote understanding among students, teachers, and parents.

2. Community Workshops: Organize workshops and seminars to educate the community about different disabilities, emphasizing the importance of inclusivity and empathy.

3. Personal Stories: Share personal stories or organize storytelling events that highlight the experiences of families with special needs individuals, fostering empathy and dispelling stereotypes.

ENCOURAGING INCLUSIVE PRACTICES:

1. Accessible Public Spaces: Advocate for and participate in initiatives that make public spaces, recreational areas, and facilities more accessible to individuals with special needs.

2. Inclusive Events: Encourage the planning of community events that consider the diverse needs of all participants, ensuring everyone can actively participate.

3. Employment Opportunities: Collaborate with local businesses to promote inclusive hiring practices, creating opportunities for individuals with special needs to contribute to the workforce.

4. Support Networks: Establish or participate in community support networks that bring together families, educators, and professionals to share resources and experiences.

By fostering understanding in the community and encouraging inclusive practices, you contribute to creating environments that celebrate diversity and provide equal opportunities for everyone, including those with special needs.

11

Technology and Special Needs:
UTILIZING ASSISTIVE TECHNOLOGIES

Utilizing Assistive Technologies:

1. Communication Devices: Explore augmentative and alternative communication (AAC) devices that assist individuals with speech or communication challenges.

2. Text-to-Speech Software: Use text-to-speech software to support individuals with reading difficulties or visual impairments.

3. Interactive Learning Apps: Leverage interactive learning apps designed for various abilities to enhance educational experiences for special needs individuals.

4. Adaptive Computer Devices: Consider adaptive computer devices, such as specialized keyboards or mouse alternatives, to facilitate computer use for those with physical disabilities.

5. Sensory Apps: Utilize sensory apps designed to provide calming or stimulating experiences for individuals with sensory processing challenges.

Navigating Digital Resources:

1. Online Support Groups: Join online communities and

support groups tailored to special needs individuals and their families to share experiences and access valuable resources.

2. Educational Websites: Explore educational websites that offer specialized content and resources catering to different learning styles and abilities.

3. Telehealth Services: Take advantage of telehealth services for remote access to healthcare professionals and therapeutic sessions.

4. Webinars and Training: Attend webinars and online training sessions focused on technology for special needs, ensuring you stay informed about the latest advancements.

5. Digital Skill Development: Introduce digital skill development opportunities, such as coding or digital art programs, to foster creativity and independence.

By embracing assistive technologies and effectively navigating digital resources, you empower individuals with special needs to enhance their communication, learning, and overall quality of life in the digital age.

12

Celebrating Milestones

Recognizing Achievements, Big and Small:

1. Create Milestone Charts: Develop visual milestone charts that highlight both short-term and long-term goals, celebrating progress along the way.

2. Personalized Rewards: Establish personalized rewards systems to acknowledge achievements, tailoring incentives to your child's interests and preferences.

3. Family Celebrations: Celebrate achievements as a family with special activities, outings, or small gatherings to create lasting positive memories.

4. Acknowledgment Rituals: Develop acknowledgment rituals, such as a "success jar" where family members write and share achievements to reflect on during challenging times.

5. Social Recognition: Share achievements with extended family, friends, and support networks, fostering a sense of community and encouragement.

Cultivating a Positive Family Environment:

1. Open Communication: Foster open and honest

communication within the family, creating an environment where everyone feels heard and supported.

2. Emphasize Strengths: Focus on each family member's strengths and unique qualities, fostering a positive and empowering atmosphere.

3. Quality Time: Prioritize quality family time, engaging in activities that promote bonding, communication, and shared experiences.

4. Encourage Individual Expression: Support individuality within the family, allowing each member, including the special needs individual, to express themselves freely.

5. Team Approach: Approach challenges as a team, reinforcing the idea that the family unit is a source of strength and support for every member.

By recognizing achievements, big and small, and cultivating a positive family environment, you contribute to a nurturing and supportive atmosphere that encourages growth, resilience, and a sense of accomplishment for all family members.

13

Individualized Service Plans (ISPs)

Introduction to ISPs

Navigating the world of special needs services can be overwhelming for many parents. One essential tool that can help streamline and personalize the support for your child is the Individualized Service Plan (ISP). This chapter will delve into what ISPs are, why they are important, where and how to obtain them, who is involved in the process, and when they should be reviewed and updated. Additionally, we will compare ISPs with Individualized Education Plans (IEPs) and provide a real-life example to illustrate their practical application.

WHAT IS AN ISP?

An Individualized Service Plan (ISP) is a document that outlines the specific services and supports a child with special needs will receive. The plan is tailored to the unique needs of the child, ensuring that they receive the appropriate interventions and services to promote their development and well-being. ISPs are comprehensive and can cover a range of services, including speech therapy, occupational therapy, physical therapy, attendant care, respite care, habilitation care, and skilled nursing care.

WHY ARE ISPS IMPORTANT?

ISPs are crucial because they provide a structured and personalized approach to meeting the needs of children with special needs. They ensure that:

- Services are tailored to the child's unique needs: Each child has different requirements, and an ISP ensures that the services provided are specific to those needs.
- Goals are clearly defined: ISPs set measurable and attainable goals for the child's development.
- Coordination among service providers: An ISP helps in coordinating the efforts of various service providers to work towards common goals.
- Accountability and monitoring: Regular reviews of the ISP ensure that the services provided are effective and that adjustments can be made as necessary.

WHERE AND HOW TO **Obtain an ISP?**

ISPs are typically developed through a collaborative process involving various stakeholders, including parents, service providers, and sometimes the child themselves, depending on their age and ability to participate. Here are the steps to obtain an ISP:

1. Assessment: The process begins with a thorough assessment of the child's needs, conducted by qualified professionals.

2. Meeting with Service Providers: After the assessment, a meeting is arranged with all relevant service providers to discuss the findings and draft the ISP.

3. Drafting the Plan: The ISP is drafted, outlining the services to be provided, the goals to be achieved, and the responsibilities of each party.

4. Review and Approval: The draft ISP is reviewed by all stakeholders, and once everyone agrees, it is approved and implemented.

5. Implementation and Monitoring: The ISP is put into action, and regular monitoring ensures that the goals are being met.

WHO IS INVOLVED **in the ISP Process?**

The development and implementation of an ISP involve a team of people, including:

- Parents or Guardians: They provide valuable insights into the child's needs and help shape the plan.
- Service Providers: These can include therapists, educators, and medical professionals who will deliver the services outlined in the ISP.
- Case Manager or Coordinator: A designated person who oversees the entire process, ensuring that services are delivered as planned and that the ISP is regularly reviewed and updated.
- The Child: Depending on their age and ability, the child may also be involved in the process of expressing their preferences and goals.

WHEN SHOULD **an ISP be Reviewed and Updated?**

ISPs are dynamic documents that should be reviewed and updated regularly to ensure they remain relevant to the child's evolving needs. Reviews are typically conducted:

- Annually: A formal review is usually scheduled once a year.

- When Major Changes Occur: If there are significant changes in the child's condition or needs, the ISP should be reviewed and updated accordingly.

- Upon Request: Parents or service providers can request a review at any time if they feel that the ISP needs adjustments.

ISP VS. IEP: **Understanding the Difference**

While both ISPs and IEPs are designed to support children with special needs, they serve different purposes and contexts:

- Individualized Service Plan (ISP):

-Scope: Covers a wide range of services beyond education, including healthcare and in-home support.

- Setting: Used in various settings, including home, community, and medical facilities.

- Purpose: Ensures comprehensive care and support tailored to the child's overall development and well-being.

- Individualized Education Plan (IEP):

- Scope: Focuses specifically on educational goals and services.

- Setting: Primarily used within the school system.

- Purpose: Ensures that the child receives appropriate educational accommodations and support to succeed academically.

. . .

REAL-LIFE EXAMPLE **of an ISP**

To illustrate how an ISP works, let's consider the story of Emily, a 7-year-old girl with cerebral palsy.

Assessment: Emily's parents noticed that she had difficulties with mobility and communication. They sought an assessment from a team of specialists, including a pediatrician, a physical therapist, and a speech therapist.

Meeting with Service Providers: Based on the assessment, a meeting was arranged with the service providers to discuss Emily's needs and draft an ISP. Emily's parents, therapists, and a case manager attended the meeting.

DRAFTING THE PLAN: **The team drafted an ISP that included:**

- Physical Therapy: Sessions twice a week to improve mobility and strength.
- Speech Therapy: Weekly sessions to enhance communication skills.
- Attendant Care: An aide to assist Emily with daily activities at home.
- Respite Care: Temporary care to give Emily's parents a break.
- Habilitation Services: Programs to help Emily develop self-care and social skills.

Review and Approval: The draft ISP was reviewed and agreed upon by all stakeholders, and then implemented.

Implementation and Monitoring: Over the next year, Emily received the services outlined in her ISP. Regular check-ins with her case manager ensured that any necessary adjustments were made. At the annual review, the team assessed Emily's progress and updated the ISP to reflect her new goals and needs.

Note: An ISP is a vital tool for ensuring that children with special needs receive the comprehensive and personalized support they require. By understanding what ISPs are, why they are important, where and how to obtain them, who is involved, and when they should be updated, parents can effectively advocate for their child's needs and help them achieve their fullest potential.

Bonus Section: Taking the Next Steps

Call 2 Action:

- Join a Support Group: Connect with local or online communities for shared experiences and advice.
- Advocate for Your Child: Get involved in your child's education and therapy plans. Attend meetings, ask questions, and ensure your child's needs are met.
- Keep Learning: Stay informed about new treatments, therapies, and educational strategies.
- Share Your Story: Your experiences can inspire and help others. Consider writing a blog, joining a forum, or speaking at events.

Advice from Other Parents, Doctors, Teachers, and Special Needs Experts

- Parents: "Patience and persistence are key. Celebrate every small victory."
- Doctors: "Early intervention is crucial. Don't hesitate to seek help and explore different therapies."
- Teachers: "Engage with your child's teachers regularly. Consistent communication can make a significant difference."

- Special Needs Experts: "Build a strong support network around your family. It's okay to ask for help."

Section for Parents

Q: What should I do if I suspect my child has special needs?

A: Start by consulting your pediatrician, who can refer you to specialists for a proper diagnosis and early intervention services.

Q: How can I prepare for an IEP/ISP meeting?

A: Bring all relevant documents, know your child's rights, and list down any questions or concerns you have.

Q: What resources are available for financial assistance?

A: Look into programs like Medicaid, SSI, and local nonprofit organizations that offer grants and aid.

Advocacy Tips

- Know Your Rights: Familiarize yourself with laws and regulations, such as the IDEA.
- Document Everything**: Keep detailed records of your

child's progress, communications with professionals, and any formal plans.

- Be Persistent: If you encounter obstacles, keep pushing for the services and support your child needs.

- Network: Join advocacy groups and connect with other parents to share resources and strategies.

Managing Behaviors

- Consistency: Establish routines and stick to them.

- Positive Reinforcement: Reward good behavior with praise and small rewards.

- Clear Communication: Use simple, clear language and visual aids if necessary.

- Seek Professional Help: Behavioral therapists can provide strategies tailored to your child's needs.

Inspirational Quotes

- "*Alone we can do so little; together we can do so much.*" – Helen Keller

- "*Every child is a different kind of flower, and all together, make this world a beautiful garden.*" – Anonymous

- "*The only disability in life is a bad attitude.*" – Scott Hamilton

Success Stories from Parents

- Jane's Journey: "When my son was diagnosed with autism, I felt lost. But through consistent therapy and support from our community, he has made incredible progress. Today, he communicates effectively and enjoys school."

- Tom's Triumph: "My daughter has Down syndrome. Early intervention and a strong IEP team have been crucial. She's now reading at her grade level and has a wonderful group of friends."

Purpose of the Book

This book was written to be a comprehensive guide and a beacon of hope for parents of special needs children. It aims to provide practical advice, emotional support, and a sense of community. By sharing our stories and resources, we hope to empower you to be the best advocate for your child.

Short Story:

How the Author of "Behind Closed Doors," Mark Taylor, Benefited from Being a Resourceful Parent

When my son Mark Jr. was born, we faced many unknowns. By seeking out resources, attending workshops, and connecting with other parents, I became more knowledgeable and confident. This proactive approach not only helped Mark receive the best possible care but also strengthened our family bond. Mark is now thriving, and I've found my passion in helping other parents navigate this journey.

Thank you for joining us in "Behind Closed Doors." Remember, every step you take, no matter how small, makes a significant difference in your child's life. Stay strong, stay informed, and continue to be the incredible parent that you are.

Sections for Parent Stories and Journeys

1. Parent Testimonials:

. . .

. . .

2. Developmental Milestones

. . .

Behind Closed Doors

. . .

3. Photographs

. . .

. . .

RESOURCE LISTINGS **and Networking**

1. Community Resources Directory

Behind Closed Doors

. . .

. . .

2. Service Providers

. . .

. . .

3. Interactive Resource Map:

. . .

. . .

PRACTICAL TOOLS **and Guides**

1. Tips and Advice:

. . .

. . .

2. Checklists and Planner Pages:

. . .

. . .

COMMUNITY BUILDING FEATURES

1. Discussion Prompts:

2. Social Media Integration:

3. Event Calendars

PERSONAL REFLECTION **and Goal Setting**

1. Reflection Pages:

2. Goal Setting Worksheets:

ADDITIONAL SUPPORT TOOLS

1. Emergency Information Page:

2. Resource Wish List:

UNIVERSAL RESOURCES **for New and Expecting Parents of Special Needs Children**

1. National Organizations:

- Easterseals
- The Arc
- Autism Speaks
- United Cerebral Palsy (UCP)
- National Down Syndrome Society (NDSS)
- National Down Syndrome Congress (NDSC)
- Parent to Parent USA

2. Government Resources:

- Individuals with Disabilities Education Act (IDEA)
- Early Intervention Programs
- Medicaid and Children's Health Insurance Program (CHIP)
- Social Security Disability Insurance (SSDI) and Supplemental Security Income (SSI)

3. Online Resources and For

- MyAutismTeam
- Special Needs Parenting Forum on Reddit
- BabyCenter's Special Needs Community

4. Educational Websites:

- Understood.org
- Wrightslaw
- LD Online

5. Books and Literature:

- "The Out-of-Sync Child" by Carol Kranowitz
- "Parenting a Child with Sensory Processing Disorder" by Christopher R. Auer and Susan L. Blumberg
- "The Special Needs Parenting Survival Guide" by Jonathan Singer

. . .

GRIEVING **Support**

1. Grieving Support Information:

- National Grief Support Organizations: Contact information for organisations such as *The Compassionate Friends* and *GriefShare*.

- Local Support Groups: Space for listing local grief support groups and counseling services.

- Books and Online Resources: Recommendations for books and websites that offer support for grieving families.

Made in the USA
Columbia, SC
08 August 2024

52683da7-6bad-4e3a-8218-539b31cd9c04R01